THE ART OF GOLDFISH KEEPING

Breeding to fix new varieties continues today in China and Japan. Chinese varieties tend to appear rather grotesque, with bulging eyes and uneven growth, but still retaining a certain beauty and charm, whereas in Japan they produce more harmonious and precise varieties. Their scrupulous methods of selection also enable them to produce goldfish of a constant and particularly high quality.

In my experience in breeding goldfish and Koi, fixing a variety is morphologically easy, since the offspring, as with humans, tend to resemble the parent to a large degree and changes are generally passed on. Difficulties do arrive, however, where fixing the colours is concerned.

Goldfish are sold everywhere in Japan, where the public is very discerning, so the quality is always of a very high standard.

3

VARIETIES AND CHARACTERISTICS

There are more than 30 established varieties of goldfish, each with its own name and specific characteristics. The genetic make-up of the goldfish proved to be very pliable, and it is for this reason that the Chinese, Koreans and Japanese have managed to establish, through careful selection and breeding of the various mutations that appeared, the fixed varieties that can be found today. As we saw earlier, the first variety is the common goldfish that originated from the crucian carp, the noticeable difference being the convex dorsal fin on the latter compared with the concave on the former and, of course, the noticeable variations in colour. Although there are now orange and red varieties of the crucian carp called 'Hibuna', neither of these fish should be confused with the common carp, *Cyprinus carpio*, from which the Japanese have produced the very colourful 'Nishikigoi' or Koi.

CHARACTERISTICS

FINNAGE

Apart from the vibrant colours, one of the most attractive features of the different varieties of goldfish is their finnage. As we have seen, there are five sets of fins, the caudal or tail fin, the anal fin, ventral fins, pectoral fins and dorsal fin. The variations in these which are common to the different varieties appear in three different manners, either shortening or increasing in length, doubling of the caudal or anal fins and, in come cases, an absence altogether of the dorsal fin.

Each consists of hard fin rays that support the soft fin membrane. If a fin ray breaks or the membrane splits it will repair itself. Unfortunately, a fin ray can develop a bud around the area where it was broken.

BODY SHAPE

By looking at the photographs between pages 22 and 53 we can clearly see the difference in body shape that varies from the long, streamlined torpedo shape of the common goldfish, Shubunkin and Comet to the rounded shapes of the Ryukin, Oranda and Buffalo Head varieties.

The compact round shapes are mainly due to the variations in the form of the backbone, which in some cases turns up at the beginning behind the head and curves down at the tail joint. This tends to compact the body and shorten the overall length of fish.

Israel also produces goldfish; many of these are Comets and Shubunkins of a good standard.

HEAD SHAPES

Heads are perhaps best described as pointed or rounded. The rounded varieties have a hood made up of fat, known as 'wen', which appears on the head and gill covers of the Oranda and Buffalo Head varieties. The fatty growth takes between two to three years to develop, with the help of special raising conditions and the right food. Generally, the more growth the better and on some examples the growth is so developed it covers the eyes.

Other features are an exaggeration of the small nose membrane that grows into an extraordinary 'narial bouquet'.

THE EYES

There are three characteristic differences in the eyes in various varieties. One is the protruding eyes of the Demekin or Telescope variety; another is the upturned eyes seen in the Celestial variety; and the third is the upturned eyes, each with a large sac filled with fluid, known as Bubble Eyes.

VARIETIES OF GOLDFISH

There are many beautiful varieties of fancy goldfish. This section of my book will give an indication of the most popular and easy to obtain. As with all varieties, a collector will look for good coloration and patterns with good head growth, body shape and finnage.

COMMON GOLDFISH
The common goldfish is one of the world's most popular pets.

Above: *Common goldfish*

Opposite: *Group of goldfish with plastic plants*

COMET

The Comet was developed in the USA. It is either red or red and white. The red and white variety are sometimes referred to as Sarassa. Their streamlined shape and fast swimming ability are not well adapted to aquarium life.

The Comet's distinctive long finnage adds elegance to its swimming motion.

The Comet variety was created in the USA during the late 19th century.
The name derived from Halley's comet, with its luminous trail.

Ryukin

The Ryukin is one of the most popular of aquarium goldfish that are kept today. The distinguishing characteristics of this variety are its round belly and long tail which can be either triple or quadruple. The original source of the Ryukin was China, but they were adopted by the Japanese and soon became very popular. The red and white variety are the most appreciated, although the calico Ryukin (base colour blue with red, white and black markings) is also beautiful. The variety is often referred to as the fringetail and has an excellent flutter to its swimming movements.

Above: *Ryukin*

Opposite: *Red and white Ryukin*

Above: *Calico goldfish*

Opposite: *Orange and white Ryukin*

SABAO

The shape of the Sabao is very similar to that of the Ryukin, but with a single caudal fin. It is a very hardy and attractive goldfish.

Sabao

BUFFALO HEAD
(Ranchu) ex. Lionhead

The original Buffalo Head came from Korea and is probably the rarest and most sophisticated of goldfish. There are shows held every year in Japan to choose a champion. The basic aspects for high appreciation and judging are a total absence of the dorsal fin, with a perfectly rounded back and symmetrical body shape. Other important values that are judged are the shape of the caudal fin, and the distribution of the 'wen' over the head and gill covers. It is apparently very difficult to breed, with a success rate as low as 30 to 40 per cent. A Buffalo Head goldfish was sold at auction in the USA in 1974 for the sum of $500,000. The only other fish to beat this record sale was a Japanese Koi that was sold for more than $850,000.

Young Buffalo Head

TOSAKIN

The main breeding centre for this particular variety is in Kochi City in Japan and it is said that it was bred from mutations that were found while breeding an Osaka Buffalo Head (a common Buffalo Head but without 'wen') with a Fringetail goldfish. The Tosakin has a very unusual and 'dainty' tail formation. It has great difficulties in swimming and prefers to remain near the bottom of the aquarium. Tosakin are best bred and appreciated in shallow containers.

Tosakin

PEARLSCALE

This variety has very unusual scales that look like half-round pearls. They can be red, red and white, calico, black, black and white or blue. The specimen in this photo is referred to as a Blue Pearlscale. It is said to have originated in China and has a very similar body shape to the Ryukin or Fringetail.

Pearlscale Fringetail

33

HANA NISHIKI

This variety is very unusual, with a ball balanced on its head. This particular specimen also has pearl scales. The origins of this goldfish have been traced back to China, but it is believed that they are now only bred in Japan.

Above and opposite: *Hana nishiki*

BUBBLE EYE

A very striking goldfish, with its huge bags containing fluid protruding from around its eyes. The bubbles are particularly fragile and easily damaged. They are susceptible to bacterial attacks which will eventually pierce the sac. As the fluid escapes the bubble will deflate, but, remarkably, if treated with care it will repair and inflate again. As with the Buffalo Head, this variety of goldfish is without a dorsal fin. There are red, orange, red and white, black and calico varieties.

Close-up of Bubble Eye

Bubble Eye calico

CELESTIAL

This variety is closely related to the Bubble Eye, but there is a noticeable difference in the shape of the eyes that are similar to those of the Telescope (Demekin) variety, but in this case they are turned upward towards the heavens. Many examples of the Celestial goldfish are metallic looking.

The Celestial goldfish is always looking upwards towards the heavens.

SHUBUNKIN

This goldfish is very similar to the Comet variety but has calico colouring. There are several different versions, the most popular being the 'Bristol Shubunkin' that has a rounded and less streamlined tail.

Above and opposite: *Shubunkin*

TELESCOPE EYE
(Demekin)

The principal feature of this goldfish is its protruding eyes and, apart from the common goldfish, Comets and Shubunkins, it is probably the most popular variety to be bred in large numbers. It is without doubt unusual and attractive. It is normally black, but red and white, and calico examples are also found. Excellent specimens have a body and tail shape similar to that of the Ryukin variety and a sail-like, very high dorsal fin that is highly appreciated.

Above: *Telescope Eye (Demekin)*

Opposite: *Panda Demekin*

43

ORANDA

Orandas are the largest of the goldfish varieties, with some specimens measuring more than 20 cm. The hooded growths of 'wen' add an attractive and almost charming look to this goldfish. Some examples can become particularly tame. As with the Ryukin, the Oranda has graceful swimming motions.

Two white Orandas

Three white Orandas in a group

Black Oranda

45

Oranda goldfish with an uprooted plant

Above: *Chocolate Oranda*

Opposite: *Head of a red and white Oranda*

Previous pages: *A red and white Oranda in an aquarium*

DUTCH CALICO
(Azuma nishiki)

This is probably one of the most colourful of the Oranda goldfish varieties.

Above: *Two calico Orandas in an aquarium*

Opposite: *Head of calico Oranda*

RED CAP ORANDA

In Japan this is a very highly appreciated variety, as it resembles the Japanese national colours and flag. It is sometimes referred to as a 'Tancho Oranda' as its cap represents the red crest on the head of the 'Tancho crane'. A prized specimen has just a red 'wen' cap perched on its head.

Above: *A red cap Oranda in an aquarium*

Opposite: *Red cap Oranda with narial bouquet*

GENETIC CHART

NAMES AND COLOURING

1 Iron-coloured Tetsugyo
2 Crucian carp – Funa (dark olive green)
3 Red-marked calico – Shubunkin (white/blue/red with black spots; blue is the base colour)
4 Watonai (golden orange)
5 Scarlet carp – Hibuna (red)
6 Peacocktail – Jikin (red fins, edge of gill cover, white body)
7 Golden Bleareye – Kinranshi (gold with black markings)
8 Common Japanese goldfish – Wakin (golden red)
9 Celestial – Chotengan (golden yellow)
10 Calico Telescope Eye (white/blue/red with black spots)
11 Buffalo Head – Rancho (golden orange)
12 Tosakin
13 Fringetail – Ryukin (red and white)
14 Red Telescope Eye – Akademekin
15 Black Telescope Eye – Kurodemekin
16 Autumn calico (golden brown, orange)
17 Iron-coloured Fringetail – Tetsu onaga
18 Marco – Maruko (golden orange)
19 Nankin (white body, orange fins)
20 Calico (orange, white spots and fins)
21 Dutch Lionhead – Oranda shishigashira (orange and white fins)
22 Osaka Buffalo Head – Osaka Rancho (red fins and head, body red and white)
23 Dutch calico – Azum nishiki (red head growth, blue and white body, white fins and black spots)

Opposite: *Goldfish genetics chart (after Dr Yoshiichi Matsui)*

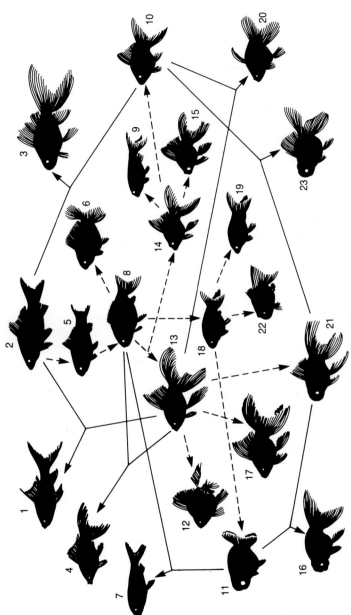

4

COLOURS

Basically coloration in fish, as with other animals, comes from a distribution of cells known as chromatophores. Rich in pigment, these can be over the skin or under the scales and are either red, yellow or black in colour. The variations in the size, intensity, distribution and superimposition of these cells, or an absence altogether of one or more of the basic tints, will make up the colours and patterns that appear on the various varieties of our goldfish. For example, the red varieties occur when there is a lack in chromatophores of black pigmentation and a fish with a total absence of chromatophores containing pigment will be determined as an albino.

The reflection of the skin and scales of fish is due to a compound known as guanine, and the more intense this is the more nacrous or pearly the skin or scales appear. Guanine can be found behind the pigmentation on the scales, or skin or can be absent altogether, giving the colours a matt appearance and in some cases making the fish appear as if it were scaleless. A white or silver variety will occur when there is a total absence of pigmentation, but there is ample guanine over the skin and/or under the scales. The colour blue, for example, is due to either a thick layer of guanine with a distribution of black pigmentation or the chromatophores containing black pigmentation appearing deeper under the skin, with very little or an absence of guanine altogether.

It is also a fact that even goldfish in their wild state have the same coloured cells as those of the domestic varieties. The difference is in the distribution of the cells, in that those of the wild goldfish are rarely in great enough concentrations to produce

The Oranda, one of the most popular varieties of fancy goldfish, can reach 30 cm in length. The characteristic wen is sometimes referred to as a hood.

vivid colours or patterns. The goldfish in its wild state has a mixture and greater quantity of black and yellow cells, thus giving an olive green or dark brown appearance. Constant cross-breeding and selection have altered the distribution and concentration of the cells in the domestic varieties.

MAINTAINING COLOUR

Coloration is influenced by many factors apart from the origin and quality of the goldfish. Feeding plays an important role, for example carotene and spirulina, substances that can be found in quality prepared foods, will help to reinforce the coloration of your goldfish. Live foods, such as fresh shrimp, and vegetables, like lettuce, will also help to maintain colours.

The colour of the common goldfish can be light orange to dark red. White varieties are referred to as albinos.

5

Aquarium or Pond – A Home for Goldfish

Goldfish can be kept in either an aquarium or a garden pond. Although common in the past, it is now not recommended to keep goldfish in a glass bowl or similar receptacle. Quite often, small goldfish will survive for quite a long period in such bowls, with regular maintenance, but it is a life of stress with brutal fluctuations in water temperatures and water chemistry, and no chance of privacy.

Within a garden pool or indoor aquarium, goldfish are very much at home. The faster-swimming, streamlined common goldfish prefer a garden pool with plants and clean water, whereas the fancy varieties prefer an aquarium environment with generously filtered water. Although the common goldfish and all their fancy varieties are of the same species, the latter variety are unable to compete for food against their faster-swimming cousins and not all fancy varieties are able to support colder winter temperatures. However, if properly adapted by being introduced in spring, stronger fish will adjust perfectly well to temperate outside conditions.

The Indoor Aquarium

An aquarium with fancy goldfish in the home is a very pleasant feature and one that is as attractive as a collection of tropical or marine fishes. It would be foolhardy to say that goldfish are easier to keep than other species of fishes, however. Although very resistant to adverse conditions, such as higher levels of pollution and low oxygen levels, it is not to be believed that because they resist better it is OK for goldfish to be kept in such an environment. As with other species, they also need good water maintenance, regular feeding and proper dissolved oxygen levels.

The basic needs to provide a decent home for your fish are very simple:

● an aquarium of large enough capacity to be able to house your future population of goldfish, leaving enough water volume so as not to overload the burden on your maintenance equipment, i.e. filter and means of oxygenation, to the point where its efficiency level will drop off rapidly at short intervals, especially when you decide to introduce extra fish or when you are not there;

● as previously mentioned, the introduction of compatible varieties, i.e. goldfish for aquariums and not for ponds;

● correct feeding and the regular maintenance that is appropriate to your particular aquarium and its accompanying equipment;

● regular interest in reading books and magazines on the subject of keeping fish – a source of finding the answers to those unanswered questions that will inevitably arrive during your adventure into the world of goldfish keeping.

It is very difficult to maintain an aquarium of 100 l or less. Goldfish are quite large, and are heavy eaters and oxygen burners, so they will produce large quantities of dissolved and solid waste products. It is advisable to opt for an aquarium of 150 l or, even better, 200 l or more.

You will need to install your aquarium on a support, either a ready-made aquarium stand or some type of furniture, or a sturdy cupboard, situated at a point as far away as possible from the nearest window, door or radiator. This will help to reduce the likelihood of the growth of algae on the aquarium glass and also possible rapid water temperature changes due to penetrating sunlight, draughts or heat from a radiator. The cupboard will not

---

To keep your goldfish in a good condition, and enjoy the countless hours of beauty and pleasure that they bring, their environment must be kept clean and care should be taken not to over-feed them.

---

only help to blend in the aquarium with the rest of your furniture, but can also serve as a place to house a filter and any other external equipment, together with such items as your air pump, cleaning material, food, nets, medicaments, books and magazines, etc. Before installing the aquarium you should check that your aquarium support is horizontal. To avoid the risk of the bottom glass cracking under the pressure of the water, the aquarium should be placed on a thin sheet of polystyrene. Also, to avoid seeing the wallpaper or any trailing pipes or wires from various accessories through the glass, the back glass of the aquarium can be painted on the outside or covered before its final installation. Ideally, use one of the readily available plastic backings that are printed with decorative photographs of plants or rocks etc. This will add more relief to the overall presentation of the inside of the aquarium.

Adding gravel to the aquarium is not only for decoration, it also provides a substrate for any plants. Before adding this, however, it is advisable to clean it thoroughly with hot water. Do not use any cleaning agents, as these could leave behind toxic residues even after a thorough rinsing. About 6 to 8 cm of gravel will be enough and this should be higher at the back of the aquarium to allow easy cleaning of any solid waste that will tend to collect at the front. However, goldfish will forage continuously and more often than not flatten out any hills or dales that you have created with your gravel. Finally, to add water to your aquarium, direct the water on to an upturned plate so as not to disturb its floor or any plants that you may have planted beforehand. Anyother decoration can also be added, such as bog wood or rocks and slate, but be sure that none of the objects will injure the goldfish and that they are not toxic.

Following two pages: *A number of gravels and sands can be used as a substrate, and to decorate the bottom of your aquarium. These must be kept clean by vacuuming when excess dirt accumulates on the surface. Failing to do this will provoke unwanted pollution that will over-burden your filter system and might harm your goldfish.*

Filtering the Water

Compared with the relatively small tropical fish, goldfish produce large quantities of waste, so some means of filtering their water must be provided. It should also be realized that the size of the filter compared to the water volume of the aquarium is not to be confused with an already established filter-to-water volume recommended by the manufacturers for the installation of an aquarium for tropical fish. Therefore, it is advisable to install a filter of a much larger volume than specified.

One goldfish can, in fact, produce 30 times more waste than an average-sized tropical fish, so this will give you some insight as to the burden imposed on your filter system. To ignore this fact will only bring you the problems caused by high ammonia and nitrite levels that you initially set out to reduce by the installation of your filter.

How do filter systems work?

Filtering the aquarium or pond water is achieved by mechanically and biologically, and/or chemically filtering the water.

Mechanical filtering uses a substrate to remove suspended material from the water to aid clarity. Biological filtering is achieved by using a material substrate to which beneficial aerobic bacteria can colonize, multiply and transform harmful dissolved organic materials, such as ammonia and nitrite, with the help of oxygen, into less harmful products. In most cases chemical filtration is achieved by using activated carbon, which removes toxic waste by absorption and once totally saturated it can be replaced. Zeolite (an absorbent mineral) is sometimes used in filter systems and this will remove ammonia directly from the water. Zeolite can be cleaned and reused by soaking in a saturated salt solution for 36 hours before being rinsed and recycled.

(*Note:* carbon should be used with caution in aquariums containing plant life, as it can partially absorb the nutrients that help to promote their growth.)

Biological filtration is the most common form of filtering

External filter systems are by far the best for positive results where filtering your aquarium water is concerned. Goldfish are great consumers of food and oxygen, and in consequence will pollute their environment very quickly. Remember, your fish are swimming in their own toilet, so you need to provide them with a suitable filter system that will be large enough to cope with their needs.

pond or aquarium water, using reticulated foam, filter wool, gravel, matting, etc. as a substrate. Some materials, for example foam, will act as a mechanical filter and also as a support for beneficial bacteria.

TYPES OF FILTER

There are many types of filter system available. Aquarium filters are either internal or external, while most garden pool filters are of the external type.

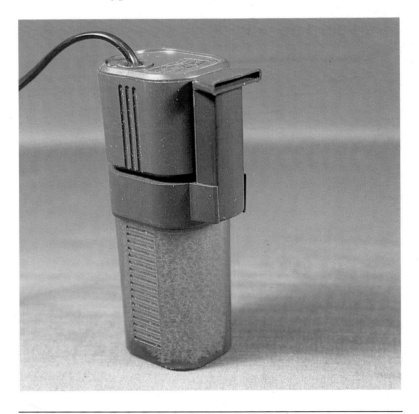

A small internal filter like this can only be used in a small aquarium with just a few small goldfish.

The most common aquarium filter (and by far the cheapest) is the 'undergravel filter' which consists of a perforated plate that is installed on the bottom of the aquarium and covered with gravel to serve as a filter substrate. The plate, or plates in the case of larger aquariums, has a plastic exhaust tube fitted in one corner. An airstone connected to an air pump is placed at the bottom of the tube and as the air bubbles formed by the stone rise, they

Filter wadding is one of the common filter substrates that is used in conjunction with other materials in external filter systems. It is very efficient in supporting helpful bacteria and retaining small particles that would otherwise return back into the aquarium. Remember to change the material at regular intervals.

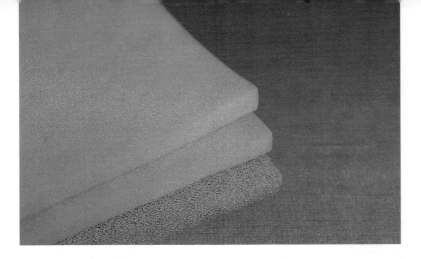

Reticulated foam is an ideal filter substrate that will retain suspended particles and also house large quantities of helpful aeroboic bacteria.

Filter matting is a relatively new filter substrate that was developed in Japan. It is particularly adapted to filters that treat large quantities of water. It is convenient because it can house a large number of helpful bacteria and requires very little maintenance.

Zeolite is used to absorb ammonia and can be regenerated so it can be used again and again.

---

pull the water through the gravel and thus create a filtering action. As this continues, aerobic bacteria form on the gravel and help purify the water.

Undergravel filters are very useful in tropical freshwater and marine aquariums, but with goldfish producing such large quantities of waste they become ineffective very quickly, as the filter action draws the waste down into the gravel which eventually becomes clogged, creating 'dead spots' that cause polluted areas. Even with regular cleaning of the gravel, using an aquarium vacuum cleaner, these systems continue to create problems for the goldfish. Plants also suffer with this type of system, as they are supplied with too much dissolved oxygen by the flow of water over their roots and any nutrients that would normally be beneficial to the plants are drawn away before they can be absorbed.

Internal filters make a better compromise, as they draw in suspended materials and can be cleaned easily at regular intervals to remove any solid waste.

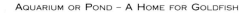

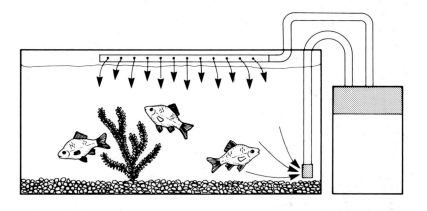

External filtration unit for a tank or aquarium

Some aquariums have their own built-in filter systems with accessories like heaters and circulation pumps.

This typical submerged pool filter will only be adequate for very small ponds containing very few fish. Where larger populations are concerned, and especially with Japanese Koi, larger, specialized filter systems are necessary.

When you are cleaning filter materials, remember that the bacteria formed on the substrate are living micro-organisms. During a cleaning operation care must be taken not to clean them away. The beneficial bacteria take several weeks to colonize your filter substrate, so if you remove them your goldfish will be subjected to high levels of dissolved toxic waste before a large enough colony of bacteria is formed again. For example, if you have reticulated foam or other substrates in your system, divide them into two and clean only half on each maintenance day (generally, once every two weeks). This will ensure that your filter will continue to function. You can also draw off a little of the aquarium water into a bucket to clean the substrate. This will avoid destruction of the bacteria by a sudden water temperature or chemistry change.

As mentioned above, biological filters rely on dissolved oxygen, so the flow of water that supplies the bacteria with oxygen must be permanent.

Nitrifying bacteria cultures for aquarium or pool use can now be obtained in liquid form. They can be added at regular intervals to help maintain a balance.

WATER CHANGES

A new aquarium set-up will obviously lack the necessary bacteria, so extra care should be taken not to over-stock or over-feed its inhabitants. Partial water changes will help keep toxic waste levels at a minimum, relieve the burden on the filter system and, in the case of a new system, give it a chance to mature.

New water of the same temperature as that of the aquarium should be added every three or four days for the first two weeks and once every two weeks thereafter during maintenance periods. About 20 per cent is enough to help keep the water chemistry right.

(*Note:* tap water usually contains additives, especially chlorine, which can be harmful to fish, so either pass the water through a dechlorinator (made from activated carbon) beforehand or simply leave the water in a container overnight in order

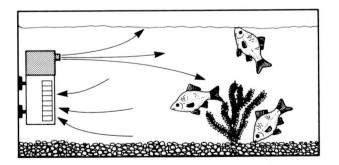

Internal filtration unit for a tank or aquarium

to let the chlorine evaporate. Aeration of the water, using an air-stone and pump, will also help a great deal in dispersing dissolved chemicals.)

It would be foolhardy to think that just any water is good enough for goldfish. The importance of filtering clearly indicates that fish are sensitive to the environment in which they live, just as humans are sensitive to atmospheric temperatures and the air we breathe.

Theoretically, water from a well, river, lake or even rainwater could be used, but this will depend on many factors, the main one being what it contains. For example, well water may be suitable for animals or even humans to drink, but it may contain dissolved or suspended elements that will prove harmful to goldfish. River water is also a risk because of pollution, whether discharged waste from a factory or chemical plant, or even the fact that the local farmer uses nitrates on his crops in the form of fertilizer. Rainwater can be used but, in most cases, depending on where the rainclouds have formed and where they have passed, it can have an acid content that is too high for goldfish.

DISSOLVED OXYGEN (O_2)

Humans require oxygen to breathe and it is exactly the same for goldfish. The difference is that the oxygen that we obtain is in the air and that of fish is dissolved in the water. In fact, there is about one-third oxygen in water compared to one-fifth in the outside atmosphere. This might seem to give goldfish an advantage, but this is not always the case, because they are kept in a given volume of water so the oxygen must be continually replaced to ensure an adequate supply.

The greatest exchange of gases takes place at the surface of the aquarium water, but, as explained earlier, we can add to the dissolved oxygen level by using an air pump connected to an airstone. To breathe, the goldfish moves water over its fine gill filaments, which transfer the dissolved oxygen to the red blood cells, which are in turn converted into energy. Because the goldfish needs to adjust its body temperature to that of the water, it uses part of the energy created to generate heat. As water and body temperatures increase, so does activity, therefore more oxygen is needed to create more energy.

Warm water contains less dissolved oxygen than cold water, so the importance of the amount of oxygen in the water increases as temperatures rise.

In a garden pool or aquarium, plants will produce oxygen by photosynthesis during light hours, while at night they will give off carbon dioxide (CO_2). Remember also that the filter system needs oxygen, so as activity increases, with breathing, eating, digesting, etc., the load on/and oxygen requirement of the filter and fish will increase. Bacteria in the tank water will increase if it becomes dirty and in turn will absorb oxygen, so we need to ensure clean water conditions.

Good aeration is indispensable in an aquarium, and small diaphragm pumps are inexpensive and cheap to run.

75

During the cold winter months an air pump will keep part of the surface free from ice to allow an exchange of the gases that are dissolved in the pond water.

WATER FLOW

The water flow rate through your system is also an important aspect to bear in mind. For example, if the water flow is too strong, the goldfish will be obliged to swim against this movement. However, as explained earlier, more gases are exchanged at the surface of the water, so a slight movement will improve this. Your filter will also have the chance to work more efficiently if the flow of water is not too strong. A good flow rate is approximately the total volume of the aquarium passing through the filter each hour.

ACID/ALKALINE CONTENT OF THE WATER

The pH scale, 0 to 14, is used to measure the acid/alkaline content of water, with 7 being the neutral measurement. As mentioned earlier, goldfish do not like water with high acid levels and, likewise, high alkaline levels produced by the excretion of ammonia will also prove extremely harmful. This, again, demonstrates the need for good filtration of the aquarium water.

WATER TEMPERATURE

Although goldfish are classed as a coldwater fish, the fancy varieties are comfortable at temperatures of between 18°C and 25°C. However, the common goldfish, Shubunkins and Comets will enjoy outside temperatures all the year round and will even stay quite comfortably at the bottom of the garden pool in a state of lethargy through the winter, even if it freezes over. In winter the warmer water becomes dense and will stay at the bottom of the pool, while the surface water freezes. If your pool has a deep area, no shallower than 80 cm, then the bottom water will remain at about 4°C. Shallow ponds may not have these areas of warmer water, so your fish could be subjected to harmful, if not fatal, variations in temperature.

Goldfish must not be fed or disturbed during their hibernating period. If you have a garden pool, your fancy goldfish could spend a few months outside during the summer. Although they are slower swimmers during surface feeding, in the height of summer they will be able to find plenty of live food in the pool which can be extremely beneficial to their health and growth.

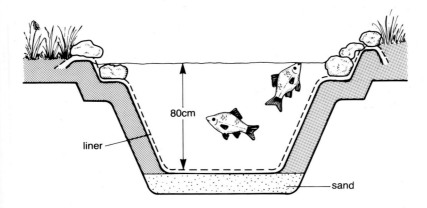

A suitable pond for keeping goldfish

Water heaters

A heater to raise the temperature of a garden pool by just a few degrees uses a large amount of costly energy and such devices are usually restricted to pools containing Japanese Koi where oil-fired or gas boilers are installed. You could buy a floating pond heater that is usually about 200 to 300 W and will only heat a small area of the water around the heater. This is quite handy for keeping a part of the surface of the pool free from ice in winter, but it can also provoke fish into swimming near the surface and thus using valuable stored energy which would be better employed in helping them through the winter months.

Heating your aquarium, however, is a simple affair using a thermostatically controlled, submersible heating element. You will have to heat the water if the temperature in the room where your aquarium is situated drops below the recommended level (4°C for pond fishes) during winter evenings. Fluctuating temperatures can be quite stressful to goldfish so it would be advisable to install a heating element in such circumstances.

A floating water heater can also be used to keep part of the pond's surface free from ice during the winter.

(*Note:* nearly all of the heaters sold today are of a solid and reliable construction, but they must never be connected, even for a few seconds, outside the water. The heaters will become warm very quickly and if placed in the water in this condition the abrupt temperature difference will cause the heater to crack and possibly leak, resulting in a high risk of electric shock.)

As with all of your equipment for pool and aquarium use, even if you think you know how it works and how to use it, take the time to read the manufacturers' instructions before installation.

And here is a final point on the subject of safety. You will not be the only person visiting your garden pool or aquarium installation. Remember, the children and a host of friends and visitors who will be coming to admire your creation. Ensure that you make all the connections correctly, installing an electrical circuit breaker and keeping everything out of reach.

AQUARIUM LIGHTING

It is essential to remember that lighting is not only for seeing what's inside the aquarium but is also as important a part of its ecological system as filtration. Many organisms depend on a light source for life, and these include your plants and fish. Plants need light to grow and to help them absorb the carbon dioxide gases that the fish produce, and your fish will need light to feel at home in their environment. For these reasons, adequate and regular lighting intervals are necessary to create a day/night rhythm.

The regularity of the lighting is of utmost importance to the fish and the plants. Irregular lighting rhythms will disrupt the plant growth and possibly stress the fish. It is advisable to install a timing device to give a regular 12- to 14-hour lighting sequence.

TYPES OF LIGHT SOURCE

For aquarium use, household tungsten-element bulbs are unsuitable because, for the amount of energy they use, they produce very little light and the energy that they do use is turned into heat which will heat the aquarium water unnecessarily. Three other types of lighting – fluorescent, mercury vapour and metal halide lamps – are adapted to aquarium systems. They are all able to produce a light source that is close to natural light, so plants and algae can use this light energy to produce food by the process of photosynthesis.

The most important characteristics of artificial lighting are its intensity and the colour spectrum of light that is produced. For example, plants need oxygen to breathe and they produce this themselves, so if the spectrum is not right and the intensity is too low, the oxygen produced during photosynthesis will be inadequate, and the plants will suffer and perhaps die. The yellow-orange and blue content of the spectrum is most important, with the blue having the most penetrating power.

Fluorescent tubes

Fluorescent tubes are the most popular light source and they are usually installed in a canopy that is placed on the top of the aquarium. They are easy to find, cheap to buy and run, and there are many different types with different light spectrums available.

Which tube to use is a matter of preference, as most are designed to produce lighting that will be beneficial to plant growth and some even enhance the colours of the fish. By experience, most aquarists use a combination of two or three types.

Fluorescent tubes are filled with different gases, such as argon and mercury vapour, that glow as an electric current passes through. The flow of current is initially produced by a starter unit that sends a high charge of electricity to the tube and, once started, the flow is regulated by a choke. Fluorescent tubes have to be replaced every six months, as their efficiency diminishes after this period. Their actual life expectancy is around 7500 hours, although some of the higher-priced models will give up to 24,000 hours. Remember that, although the tube may appear to be working quite normally, its efficiency will eventually drop off after a certain period and the undetectable difference can prove fatal to your aquarium plants.

Mercury vapour/metal halide

These lamps are also a popular light source for aquariums and are an alternative to fluorescent tubes. They generate a very high intensity light with a spectrum close to that of natural light, but they lack the intensity of blue light in the spectrum that is necessary for marine aquariums with plants and invertebrates. In these cases, it will have to be supplied by additional fluorescent tubes that emit a high level of blue light.

Mercury vapour and metal halide lamps also need to be well ventilated, and therefore have to be suspended above the aquarium.

INTENSITY OF LIGHTING

The most common fault in aquarium lighting is its intensity. It is always natural to think that just one fluorescent tube is enough, as it usually looks as if it is lighting up the aquarium quite well, but, in fact, one tube will at the most provide only 30 per cent of the lighting required by the plants. Light has a hard job penetrating water, so by the time it reaches the plants, it has lost a lot of its power. A general rule for calculating how much lighting will be required for your aquarium is to allow 30 to 40 W per ft^2 of its surface.

PLANTS

Plants are not only decorative; in some cases they are essential to complete and create an ecological balance in a garden pool or aquarium. Most fish prefer a planted-out aquarium where they can find shade and privacy if they need it, and plants also play an important role in spawning and protecting young fish. Growing plants break down carbon dioxide gas and other waste products produced by fish respiration and decomposing detritus. Plants use carbon to build new cells and give off oxygen during the process of photosynthesis, while the waste matter is turned into nitrates which act as fertilizers for the plants themselves.

Adding plants to your aquarium requires a certain degree of

forethought. For instance, goldfish forage around the tank all the time and can cause havoc by uprooting or pulling off plants' leaves. This means that only the stronger varieties of plants can be introduced. More advice on these can be obtained from your local aquatic dealer, but plants like *Elodea canadensis*, *Caeabomba*, *Ludwigia Sagittaria*, *Vallisneria* and *Myriophyllum* will all grow well in aquariums containing goldfish.

It is a good idea to introduce your plants at the same time as you set up your aquarium, providing them with a layer of nutritious substrate before adding gravel. To help provide sufficient anchorage for the roots, a piece of fine plastic netting can be placed over the substrate. To stop them from floating, some plants might need the help of small lead weights to hold them

Goldfish can uproot and generally create havoc in an aquarium containing plants. It is better only to introduce the stronger varieties.

down, but care should be taken to attach these carefully so as not to damage the stems or roots while fixing them. Threading the roots through the netting can produce an excellent result. Potted plants can also be introduced. While handling the plants, do not allow them to dry out.

While planting, some form of continuity should be aimed for. For example, the taller plants should be placed at the ends and towards the rear of the aquarium, and the smaller ones towards the front. Care should also be taken to keep them grouped: for example, bunches of five or six of the same variety will have more effect than the same number being spread out. Be sure to provide adequate swimming space for the fish.

A running-in period of a few weeks before introducing your fish will give the plants a chance to settle down in their new environment. Plant fertilizers will help a newly planted aquarium or cuttings to root and also help to maintain your plants in perfect condition. Fertilizers can come in liquid form and the recommended dose should be introduced to start with and a little added after every water change. Fertilizers also come in tablet form, containing iron and CO_2 which is absorbed by the plants. This is also a good method as long as you respect the correct dose. When buying your plants, be sure to choose only those that have vigorous root growth and are free from black or brown patches on their leaves.

6

FEEDING

Goldfish are omnivorous, feeding on both plant and animal matter, and they need a well-balanced diet in order to grow and remain healthy. For this they will depend upon their environment, but also upon their keeper to a great extent.

Fish require correct amounts of good-quality food containing essential ingredients, consisting mainly of proteins, carbohydrates, fats, vitamins and minerals. Certain of these can be stored by the fish and used as required, but many need to be consumed regularly: for example, the proteins (amino acids) that are used in building tissues. Likewise, not all vitamins can be stored successfully: an example being vitamin C, which is essential for good health in fish as well as humans. In a well-planted-out garden

Processed floating pellet food containing elements extracted from pure cultured spirulina – an ideal natural colour enhancer.

pool, goldfish will be able to feed upon vegetable matter and live foods, but depending on the size of the fish population, these might have to be supplemented by another food source. In an aquarium, however, your goldfish will rely entirely on you for their dietary needs.

There are two main foods that are available, namely prepared foods and live foods. Live foods are by far the best, but it can be difficult to have a constant supply of these. There are many preparations that are available for goldfish and, although it is debatable, continuous feeding on prepared food *can* provide an adequate supply for all dietary needs, providing, of course, that there is plenty of variation in these.

PREPARED FOODS

There are many different types of prepared foods available, ranging from floating and sinking granules to flakes and freeze-dried preparations. If you are using any of these, you must remember that the same menu can become a monotonous diet that could possibly result in complications like constipation, which is seen quite often with fancy goldfish. It is also important to remember that fish are omnivorous and that in the wild they eat vegetable matter. You should occasionally provide either fresh, chopped lettuce or spinach, or readily prepared vegetable food, if available. Remember that prepared foods have a limited storage time.

LIVE FOODS

Live foods are essential to maintain healthy fish, providing all and more of the important nutrients that are not available in prepared foods. They also aid digestion in the intestinal tract, which could be the remedy for a fish that has become constipated from being fed constantly on prepared foods.

Live foods – such as white enchytrae worms, tubifex worms, blood worms, earthworms, daphnia and brine shrimps – can all be obtained on a regular basis from your local pet shop, which will also have a supply of frozen foods. Raw meat and shrimp are also an excellent treat for your fish as long as they are thoroughly washed beforehand.

(*Note:* Live foods should never be collected from wild sources. Not only might you be breaking the law, but you could be accidently introducing unwanted organisms, such as water enemies and diseases, into your aquarium or pond.)

HOW MUCH FOOD?

This is a leading question, to say the least, and one which will take many a neophyte along the path to problems. Not only is a balance in content of diet required but also a balance in quantity. It is not so hard to calculate and is easy to remember, but difficult to achieve.

Processed floating pellet food containing the necessary nutrients and a high protein level (45 per cent) to promote growth and body shape. This is especially essential where the Oranda and Buffalo Head varieties are concerned.

The growths on the heads of the Oranda or Buffalo Head varieties are known as 'wen' (calico Oranda).

Dried daphnia is the most common of all goldfish foods and, although it can be a maintenance diet, it will not provide enough nutrients to keep a goldfish healthy.

Cultured blood worms are a real treat for your goldfish, but be careful of their origin, for, as with other live foods gathered from a wild source, they can introduce parasites and disease.

Basically, goldfish will eat as much as you feed them but will benefit from just a small amount, the rest simply passing through their digestive system and ending up as waste. Of course, watching your fish feed is a marvellous sight and it is easy to forget that the distribution of food has a precise function in maintaining a balance in the ecological system that you have created. Too much food will produce high levels of nitrite and ammonia which will place a burden on the filter system, lower the water quality and eventually put the health of your fish at risk. The golden rule is **do not over-feed** and only give a quantity than can be consumed completely within a few minutes. If any excess food is left, you should keep on removing it until you can calculate the right amount. It is easier to do this with floating food, remembering that food that sinks to the bottom of the tank or pond will not always be eaten immediately.

The frequency of feeding should be at the least once or twice a day, preferably morning and afternoon. Goldfish are coldwater fish, which means that their metabolic rate is governed by the temperature of the water. This means that if the temperature is down – say for a pond at 10°C and an aquarium at 13°C – then they will digest their food very slowly, so they should only be fed once a day, in the morning. If the temperature is up – for example, 18°C – they should be fed twice a day.

(*Note:* In a temperate zone, pond fish should not be fed during the winter months when water temperatures decline below 10°C, even on the odd warm day when they might be seen swimming around. In such regions the distribution of food should start gradually during March or April, remembering, of course, that the metabolic systems of the fish will take some time to become active again.)

HOLIDAYS

Fish can survive for long periods without food, so if you decide to go away on holiday for a week or two, you will not have to make any plans for feeding. If, however, you are taking a long holiday (more than two weeks), it would be advisable to arrange for a friend or neighbour to visit regularly and feed your fish. At the same time it would also be a good idea to instruct them in what to do if any problem arises while you are away. Essentially and most importantly, you should carry out your regular maintenance schedule a day or two before leaving. As your friend or neighbour will probably be a novice at fish keeping, it would be a good idea not to leave the supply of food at hand, but instead prepare small packets, each containing the correct daily ration.

When regular intervals are of the utmost importance in their feeding programme, an automatic feeder will be beneficial to your goldfish during your absence. Most feeders are not harmed by humidity, but you should clean the food compartments regularly and after use.

7

BREEDING

If you are fortunate enough to have a selection of goldfish in a well-planted-out garden pool, you may be lucky enough to spot a few new baby goldfish each year. Although there are usually many offspring born during the breeding season, very few survive either being eaten by other aquatic life or even by the parents themselves. The survivors are those who remain in good health and find plenty to eat, stay alert and keep hidden until they are not at risk from predators and can join the rest of the fish group. This is, of course, all part of the process of natural selection, leaving the strongest of the species to continue the life cycle.

Good specimens of all varieties of goldfish are the results of human intervention and without our continual efforts to improve them, we would not have the number of beautiful examples that there are today.

The characteristics of the parent fish are passed on to the children, so to get the best results both males and females should be carefully selected by the breeder. They should be healthy, with good body shape, regular scales and good finnage. The males should be two years old and the females three years old to get the best results. Females can usually breed at two years old, but at three or four you will get better results.

Sexing a fish is sometimes difficult, but during the breeding season there is a visually noticeable difference. With the common goldfish the males are always streamlined in shape, whereas the females develop a round abdomen as the ovaries produce eggs. The anal region of the male is more prominent than that of the female during the breeding season and the soft abdomen of the female will become firm before spawning. In most cases this occurs just once in the year. With other varieties it is sometimes more difficult to sex the fish, but you may notice that the males develop small white round tubercles on their gill covers (operculum) and on the leading edge of their pectoral fins. These hard growths are about the size of a pin-head and are sometimes referred to as pearl organs or coursing stars. They are used during the spawning act to provoke the female into releasing her eggs. If you are not sure how to sex fish, either ask for expert advice or buy at least five individuals to be reasonably sure that you have males and females.

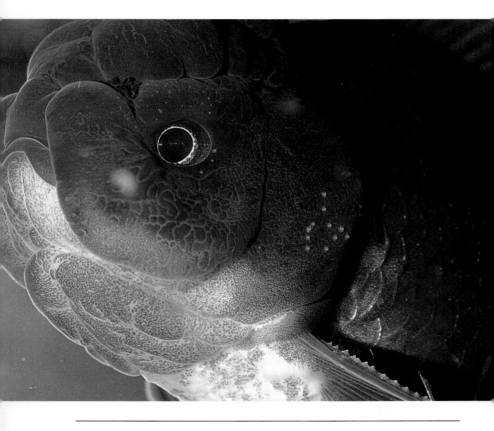

With the abdomens of the female goldfish firm, swollen with eggs, the males develop hard white tubercles, sometimes referred to as 'coursing stars', on the operculum and leading edge of the pectoral fins. During the spawning chase, the male pushes these against the female's belly to inspire her into laying her eggs.

BREEDING FISH IN POOLS

Breeding will start during the warmer months of the year as water temperatures reach 18°C. This can be from May until October in a temperate region. To prepare your fish, it is a good idea to feed them on live foods, like clean chopped earthworms, for a few weeks before you wish them to spawn. During spawning, eggs will be sprayed out by the female, while the male presses himself against her abdomen and releases his sperm, known as milt, in order to fertilize them. The eggs – approximately 1 mm in diameter, adhesive, transparent and amber in colour – will become attached to the roots and leaves of nearby plants. Females always spray their eggs near the surface, so border plants and grasses that hang in the water will collect the eggs. Floating plants, such as *Pistia stratiotes* or *Eichhornia crassipes*, are particularly attractive to spawning goldfish. Submerged plants will also support eggs and in emergencies soft conifer branches can be placed in the water around the edge of the pool.

Any eggs that are not fertilized will turn milky white within a few hours and possibly become covered in a white fungus growth by the following day. Where possible, these dead eggs

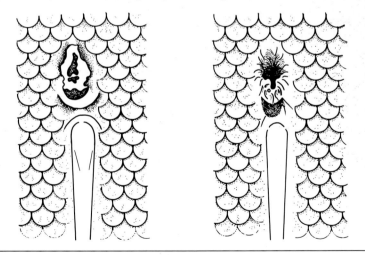

The reproductive orifice of the male (right) is smaller than that of the female.

As the female sprays her eggs on nearby plants, the male releases sperm to fertilize them.

should be removed, but care must be taken so as not to throw away good ones. An average-sized female will lay aproximately 2000 to 5000 eggs in one day, from the early hours of the morning until early afternoon. By then, with the continuing spawning chase, she will be seen resting, exhausted, on the bottom of the pool.

If you wish to raise your young goldfish, you can remove the eggs to a separate pool or tank. This must be done with care, as

The good eggs are transparent and amber in colour, and for every egg that you find there are hundreds that you do not see.

Bad eggs are opaque and eventually become covered in fungus. It is better to remove these to avoid contaminating the fertile eggs.

Below: *For the thousands of eggs that are successfully fertilized in a natural environment, very few will develop into baby goldfish. They are immediately vulnerable to predators, such as the parents themselves or other fish, who will feast on them. Look carefully and you will the see the goldfish fry inside the egg. Once the reflection of the eyes becomes apparent, hatching will commence within approximately 24 hours.*

Opposite: *Eggs that are found in the pond can be put into an aquarium to develop. The water temperature must remain stable, and the aquarium clean and free from rotting debris.*

96

they can be damaged by an abrupt change in temperature. A submerged bucket or bowl will be an ideal receptacle in which to retrieve and transfer the eggs.

BREEDING FISH IN AQUARIUMS

Goldfish will also spawn in an aquarium or a tank of about 1 m long by 30/40 cm wide, containing a 25 cm depth of water. It is necessary to clean the tank thoroughly, fill it with fresh water and aerate two days before you wish your goldfish to spawn. Floating plants or spawning grass should be arranged at each

Once hatched, the goldfish fry will cling to the plants or aquarium glass.

end of the tank, with swimming space in between and submerged plants anchored down by weights to catch the eggs that
fall to the bottom.

Where possible, the parent fish can be separated some days
beforehand. As mentioned before, water temperatures of around
18°C will influence the time of spawning, so it will be necessary
to monitor the tank temperatures. A 2 or 3°C fluctuation in temperature can stimulate spawning. This can often be seen at the
end of the summer season, in September or October, after a
severe drop in atmospheric temperatures during the night. These
conditions can be reproduced in a tank by using a thermostatically controlled heater to raise the temperature or by adding cold
water to lower the initial temperature. The afternoon is a good
time to raise the temperature and the evening is the best time to
lower it.

The parents must be introduced into the tank during the afternoon, at around 2 or 3 o'clock. The parents will start to eat the
eggs shortly after spawning so, if a tank is being used, the parents
can be returned to the pool or the plants in a pond moved to a
suitable tank containing water of the same temperature.

This is natural spawning, as in general it is not recommended
to stimulate spawning by artificial methods.

INCUBATION

The period of incubation varies from three to four days at the
ideal temperature of around 19 to 21°C to a week or longer at a
lower temperature. Longer incubation periods will produce a
higher percentage of deformed fry. The temperature can be main-
tained by using a heater and a cover over the top of the aquarium, and this will also prevent dirt and dust from falling into the
tank.

It is necessary to maintain the water quality by constant light
aeration and by removing regularly any sunken organic matter
that collects on the bottom of the tank. This should be done with
care, so as not to remove any eggs or fry.

Once the reflective tissue of the eyes of the fry can be seen in

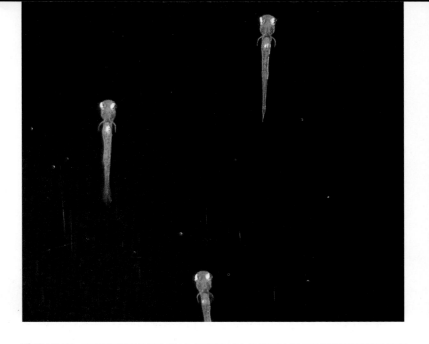

With the aid of a magnifying glass we are able to see the rudimentary pectoral fins that will help the fry to become mobile.

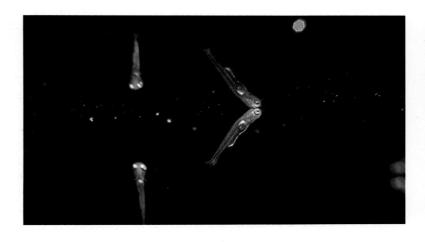

Once free-swimming, the fry will fill their swimbladders with air at the surface of the aquarium.

the egg, they will hatch after about 24 hours. When free from the egg case the 4- to 5-mm long fry will cling to the plants or walls of the aquarium and absorb the contents of their yolk sac. After two days they will have filled their swimbladders with air, developed rudimentary pectoral fins and become free-swimming in the search for food.

FEEDING THE FRY

The breeder will now be responsible for feeding the fry. A goldfish fry diet can consist of powdered egg yolk, plankton, infusoria or liquid fry food.

At this stage, they will only be able to eat very minute organisms living in the water. This can be achieved by introducing infusoria, a group of single-celled animals that can be found in water containing decomposing vegetable matter. A good supply of these can be found in stagnant water, but with the risk of introducing unwanted or dangerous organisms as well, it would be better to use commercially prepared infusoria or produce them yourself. They will be required in quantity and must be produced by the hobbyist in advance to meet the demands of the hungry fry. At water temperatures of 18 to 20°C, a developing culture can be started a day or two after the fish spawn.

Infusoria culture can be produced by placing three or four lettuce leaves or other vegetable matter into a glass jar containing water that has been brought to the boil. Crush the leaves a little and add the water carefully in order not to crack the jar. Once cooled, the jar should be covered and placed in a warm, sunny place, a window sill for example, for approximately three days, by which time the infusoria will have developed in sufficient numbers. To feed these to the fry, just pour some of the water from the jar into the tank periodically. After two or three days the culture will die and perhaps be replaced by harmful bacteria, so a second culture should be started two or three days after the first. For convenience, three cultures can be developed and date marked, with each becoming mature at intervals of two or three days.

THE ART OF GOLDFISH KEEPING

The tricky part of this feeding method is in calculating the right amount of infusoria to feed to the fry. If you do not feed enough you will possibly starve some of the fry, and too much liquid containing the culture could pollute the tank water. It is also very important to keep the infusoria alive long enough for the fry to eat, so once developed the culture must be kept at the same temperature as that of the nursery tank. It is vital to keep the tank clean: this can be carried out by using a small siphoning tube, but be careful not to remove any fry inadvertently.

At approximately one week old, the fry will be able to eat larger animals, such as daphnia, cyclops or baby brine shrimps (*Artemia salina*). Brine shrimp eggs can be found in most pet stores specializing in fish and these can be hatched very easily. There are a few ready-made brine shrimp hatcheries available to the hobbyist and these are not expensive, but you can use a jar or other convenient receptacle containing 1 l of water and a large teaspoon of natural salt. Add one level teaspoon of brine shrimp eggs and aerate vigorously, using an airstone and pump. At 20°C the eggs will hatch in about two days, while at higher temperatures they will hatch in one to two days. To feed these to the fry, remove the airstone and allow the baby shrimps, known as *nauplii*, to settle to the bottom of the jar, where they can be siphoned off by using a small tube and fed to the fry. As with your infusoria culture, several brine shrimp hatcheries can be started at different intervals to ensure a permanent supply of baby brine shrimps.

At three to four weeks old, the fry will be able to accept fine powdered fish food that can be found at your local pet shop. Feed this sparingly but regularly, little but often. During the first four weeks the fry will have to be fed three times a day and for the following four months only twice a day. After this initial period they can be fed as adult goldfish, just once a day.

SELECTION

If your fry thrive on the diet you have given them, you will have to think about the problem of space. An experienced breeder will be thinking about this during the early stages of the development of the fry and also the fact that goldfish are bred for viewing. The expert will start to select the fry at approximately two weeks old, when they would be about 1 cm long or when the shape of the tail is discernible. This gives more space to those fish of better quality for a good growth rate. The basics of selection change from variety to variety, and the fry change in colour and body shape often during their development, so more selection will produce better results. At the first selection, the most important aspect of the fry would be their caudal fin and the second selection should concern their body shape. Many deformations in caudal fin shapes can appear over a period of time – with them being either squashed, bent, only open on one side, too small or too big. The body shape should be symmetrical.

COLOUR

The colours of the goldfish will appear at different times during their growth and according to their specific variety, some after a month or two and others after six months or more. For example, common goldfishes stay with their dark olive green or brown robe for months and suddenly they will turn a dark matt blue-black before changing to golden-orange or red. Certain common goldfish can stay with their natural camouflage for years, only to change when placed in another environment.

To illustrate how selection works, with red and white goldfish only those that have these colours present should be kept, after which those that have a symmetrical pattern or colour on each side, on the mouth and on both gill covers can be selected. An absence of design or colour is just a bad quality fish.

To help the goldfish to develop their colours, they should be fed at regular intervals on live foods and their water should be kept as clean as possible and changed regularly. Prepared food containing colour enhancers must be used with caution, for example food containing carotene will help develop the reds but may turn the whites pink. Natural foods are by far the best method of feeding and developing colour. Spirulina, an algae, can be found in prepared food and is quite good for developing all colours. As mentioned before, there are also special foods to help with the development of the head growth, known as 'wen', on the Oranda and Buffalo Head varieties.

CONCLUSION

A rigorous selection from one spawning could leave you with just a few goldfish, but think how much more rewarding it will be to admire five beautiful home-bred fish than 50 ugly ones.

The Chobi variety is quite difficult to obtain. This particular example has a good pattern and body shape with exceptional coloration.

8

DISEASES AND TREATMENT

It is an unfortunate fact that goldfish, like cats and dogs, can become ill. This section will help you to look out for signs of disease in your fish and at the same time help you to administer the current treatment to bring about a cure.

DISEASES

By feeding your fish correctly and keeping their environment clean, you will avoid most problems with disease, but there is always a risk. For example, lack of oxygen, stress, rapid temper-

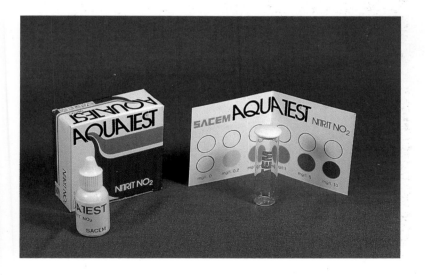

Checking on the nitrite levels in your pond or aquarium with a simple test kit will enable you to keep the water and your goldfish in perfect condition.

ature changes, an over-populated pool or aquarium, or the accidental introduction of disease from an outside source, can all be responsible for any problems that occur.

Fish can suffer from a number of diseases, but the first problem to look out for is stress. Just as stressed humans are prone to infection by bio-aggressors, so are fish, but in their case it is one of the principle causes of disease, which is all the more reason to keep your fish in a healthy environment and treat them with great care.

An early diagnosis and swift treatment are very important factors in improving your chances of curing any disease successfully. There are bascially three common diseases that can manifest themselves, namely parasite infestation, bacterial infection and fungal infection. These organisms are always present in an aquatic environment, and the immune systems and protective mucus coating of the fish are the principal defences that will ward them off, but if weakened by bad conditions like stress or damage, the risk of infection or infestation is high. Many of these organisms are opportunists and will profit when the situation is right for them. Other parasitic organisms, when present, are able to choose their victim without too much of a problem but they can be totally eliminated with the right treatment.

PARASITES

Common parasites
The common parasites of freshwater fish are known as protozoa, single-celled animals that live on the skin or gills of fish. They are *Trichodina*, *Chilodonella*, *Costia* and *Ichthyophtirius multifiliis* (white spot disease), and all can be eliminated by using the same kinds of treatment.

A goldfish infested by these parasites can be seen scratching on objects, or the bottom or sides of the tank or pool, as the infestation starts to irritate it. It can be seen flicking its fins, or possibly resting or swimming in a listless manner, with all of its fins closed, as it becomes stressed by the effects of the disease. At advanced stages the fins become quite ragged and red blotches reveal the areas where the parasites have damaged blood vessels.

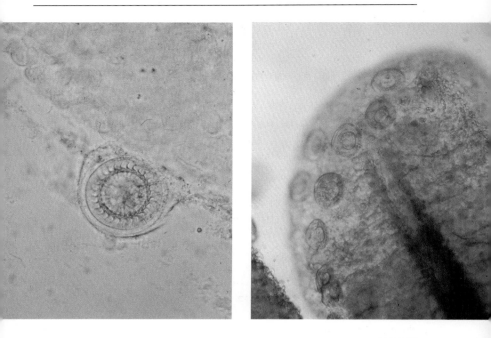

Left: *As with other external parasites,* Trichodina *on the skin will cause irritation. Diameter 50 microns.*

Right: *Parasite infestation or bacterial infection of the gills will cause respiratory difficulties. This is* Trichodina *on a gill filament.*

If the gills are infested they will become pale and swollen, and by then the fish will have developed difficulties in breathing and will eventually be seen gasping at the surface in order to secure oxygen. An infested fish could also appear thin.

Apart from the above diagnosis, an infestation of *Trichodina* can cause the skin to peel off on certain areas of the fish, especially on the gill covers and head region.

Chilodonella will not only make the fins appear ragged, but also produce white, opaque, congested areas on the fish.

A heavy infestation by *Costia* can cause an excess of mucus to be produced, which will appear as a milky slime over a large area of the body.

Ichthyophtirius multifiliis (white spot) is the most common of fish parasites and is probably responsible for more deaths than any other parasite. It will affect not only coldwater fishes, but also many tropical species. White spot is highly contagious, and can be easily transmitted from tank to tank on plants, aquarium decor and, above all, on nets. Because of this risk, nets should always be disinfected after use and, where possible, thoroughly dried.

The parasite buries itself in the skin, gill and fin membranes, where it will develop and eventually appear on the surface of the victim as small white dots, sometimes making the fish appear as

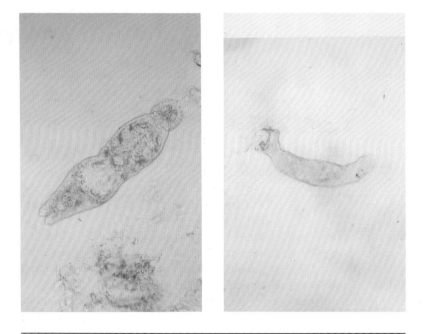

Left: Gyrodactylus *attaches itself by using two principal hooks.*

Right: Dactylogyrus *attached to a gill filament (note eye spots).*

if it were sprinkled with salt. At the last stage of the evolution the white dots fall off the fish and divide into hundreds of single cells, ready to invade another fish. As with most parasites, the life cycle of white spot is governed by water temperatures. For example, at 8°C it will take approximately two months to develop and at 25°C just five days.

Gyrodactylus and *Dactylogyrus* are monogenetic trematodes and are sometimes referred to as flukes. *Gyrodactylus* are usually found attached and feeding on the soft fin membranes or skin and *Dactylogyrus* on the gill filaments of the fish. Erosion of the fins and difficulties in breathing can reveal these parasites. *Gyrodactylus* are viviparous, producing their young, one at a time, fully developed. If a smear of mucus, or piece of gill or fin membrane is examined under a low-powered microscope, it is quite easy to find these parasites and see the young in a parent *Gyrodactylus*. *Dactylogyrus*, however, are not viviparous and have four black eye spots

Larger parasites

Lernaea, Argulus and *Ergasilus* are the larger of the common fish parasites, and can easily be spotted by the naked eye.

Lernaea, known as the anchor worm, is seen as a small splinter sticking out from underneath a scale, usually on the sides or back region of the fish. The anchor worm goes through several changes in its life cycle and at its free-swimming larval stage will install itself under a scale of the fish, where it will grow into an adult. At this stage it attaches itself by burying its anchor-shaped head under the skin of the fish. In some cases, the area around the attached worm will become reddened and perhaps swollen as bacteria infect the wound made by its penetration. It is only the female parasite who will parasitize the fish in order to develop and release her eggs. These can be seen in two elongated egg sacs at the extremity of the worm. The life cycle of the anchor worm ends as the female dies and begins again as the eggs hatch out in the water. Some fish can support a number of worms, but will eventually become weakened by their effects.

Argulus is recognized as a small, round transparent animal busily moving about and feeding on the skin of the fish. To

Despite the precautions taken with treatments and quarantine, some imported goldfish may have the larval stage of the anchor worm under one or two of their scales. These will develop into adults while the fish is in your pond or aquarium. Anchor worms can easily be spotted as a transparent splinter sticking out from underneath a scale.

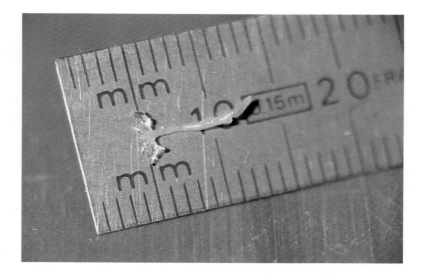

The adult anchor worm has two egg sacs attached to its posterior.

obtain its meals, it inserts a thin, hollow stylet into the skin of the fish, where it excretes a substance to dissolve body tissues and fluid before drawing them up through the stylet. Known as the fish louse, *Argulus* is a strong swimmer and is therefore able to swim from fish to fish by rapid movement of its eight crab-like legs. As with the anchor worm, it develops eggs in two sacs that are attached to its rear. Goldfish that have fish lice will sometimes display erratic behaviour in trying to free themselves from the irritating effects of the parasite.

Ergasilus, or gill louse, is a gill parasite, hooking itself on and feeding on the gill plates. It can be recognized by the small white 'V' shapes on the gills, the 'V's being the egg sacs attached at the posterior of the parasite. As it feeds on the gill lamels, the affected goldfish will develop swollen gill plates and problems in breathing.

When treating for anchor worm, fish lice or gill lice, special precautions should be taken to eliminate all stages of their development that will take place over a period of several weeks.

BACTERIA

Bacteria are difficult to identify, but there are at least four common strains that affect goldfish. The most important aspect for the hobbyist is to recognize whether or not bacteria are responsible for any disease. Bacteria infections not only make the fish weak, but can also erode the fins, gills or skin. Reddened areas around the mouth, fin joints or on the body will reveal a bacteria infection. If the gills become infected, they will appear to be pale and swollen. A lack of oxygen and dirty water with suspended debris are common causes of infection. Open wounds or stress caused by parasite attack, or damage through rough handling, will also leave the goldfish vulnerable to harmful bacteria.

ULCERS

Ulcers will appear on the sides of the fish as the scales fall off and the skin dissolves. This is partly the result of parasite attack and bacteria infection. Certain ulcers can result from severe bacterial

Hole disease is usually the result of parasite and bacteria attack, and a lack of maintenance.

infection that will manifest these effects from the insides of the fish. Again, dirty conditions will provoke this type of disease, so when treating the ailment, a thorough cleaning of the environment of your fish and rigorous inspection of your pool or aquarium equipment will help prevent any recurrence.

FUNGUS

Fungus or *Saprolegnia* will attach itself on the surface of the skin or gills of the fish as a growth that looks like cotton wool. It is common to see this appear on pool fish in spring as the water warms. It usually attacks those that have been weakened by the effects of the winter period. As with bacteria, fungus will profit from bad water conditions and can even grow on sunken debris or uneaten food. Pools that have been cleared of debris before the winter and have had a partial water change are generally free from this sort of problem. It is quite rare to see fungus appear in an aquarium.

HYDROPSY

Hydropsy or dropsy causes an area of the goldfish to swell and its scales start to stick out. Very rapidly, all of the fish can take on this pinecone effect. It is caused by dirty water conditions which occur through poor water maintenance. As contaminated fluids multiply under the skin of the fish, the swelling increases and eventually the fish will develop difficulties in breathing. It will possibly display erratic swimming behaviour before eventually dying. Dropsy is a very difficult problem to cure.

SWIMBLADDER DISORDERS

The swimbladder enables the fish to govern and stabilize its depth in the water. Any disorder in these organs will cause the goldfish to have difficulties in ascending or descending. A constipated fish, for example, could develop this problem as the gut swells and causes malfunction by pressing against the swimbladder.

CONSTIPATION

This is a common problem in many varieties of goldfish. The main reason for its appearance is a poor diet. Live foods are very important for intestinal transit, so if your goldfish appears to be constipated, feed it live food, such as chopped earthworms or conceal a grain of Epsom salts in a small piece of chopped meat. If this fails, place the fish in a container with about 10 cm of water in which 5 g of natural salt per litre has been dissolved. Raise the water temperature by 2 to 3°C using an aquarium heater, until the fish relieves itself. Disconnect the heater and remove the fish to its aquarium after the water has resumed its initial temperature.

TREATMENT

Sometimes it is difficult to treat a sick fish and success is mainly due to experience and the strength of the constitution of the fish in the case of a serious problem. While carrying out a treatment it is of utmost importance to avoid stressing the fish and to follow the instructions to the letter, especially where measuring chemicals and exposure times are concerned. Treatments are carried out either as a short-term bath in a receptable outside the pool or aquarium, or as a long-term treatment within the pool or aquarium. Antibiotics that are used in certain treatments are administered by mixing them in food.

(See the conversion table on page 6.)

MEDICINES

The medicines mentioned in this book are those which are generally used by professionals in pisciculture. There are other medicaments available for treating the same diseases that have been manufactured especially for the hobbyist.

(*Note:* All medicines should be handled with great care and the necessary precautions taken where indicated. They should also be stored and locked away out of the reach of children and animals.)

Formalin
Toxic, do not inhale. Sold commercially as 40 per cent formaldehyde solution. Used against parasite infestations as follows.

Short-term bath (30 minutes)	1 ml per 5 l of water
Long-term pool treatment	15 ml per 1000 l
Long-term aquarium treatment	1.5 ml per 100 l

(*Note:* All short-term baths should be aerated. During hot weather, formalin can induce oxygen depletion, so it is important to provide additional aeration.)

Malachite green (zinc-free) oxalate
Used to treat fungal growth and, in combination with formalin, against certain parasites.

Topical application	0.1 per cent solution
Short-term bath	2 ppm for 1 hour
Long-term pool or aquarium	
treatment	0.2 ppm

Malachite green comes in powder form, and to obtain the correct ratios needed for treatment by using ordinary letter scales, apply the following method:

● Measure out 10 g of malachite green and mix well with 1 l of water.

● Use this solution as follows:
short-term bath at 2 ppm, 1 ml of the solution per 5 l of water
long-term pool or aquarium treatment at 0.2 ppm, 20 ml per 1000 l of pool water or 2 ml per 100 l of aquarium water.

For 0.1 per cent solution for topical applications (used for removing fungus or applying to ulcers), mix 1 ml with 9 ml of water.
(*Note:* Wear rubber gloves when using malachite green.)

Sodium chloride (natural salt)
Ideally used in a convalescent tank at 25 g (2 teaspoons) per 5 l of water (4–24 hours). This is particularly helpful after treating badly affected fish with formalin. Also used to treat hydropsy or fry for bacteria, parasites or fungus.

Longer treatment can be made by siphoning off a quarter of the tank water every day, cleaning the bottom and replacing the water with clean fresh water at the same temperature as that of the tank, adding each time 25 g (2 teaspoons) of natural salt per 5 l of water in the tank. Following these procedures will build up and maintain the saline solution. On the fifth day, replace half of the solution with clean, fresh water and on the sixth day return the goldfish to their pool or aquarium.

Metrifonate

This insecticide is also known as Dipterex 80 Dylox or Neguvon. The recommended dose can be used to treat all varieties of goldfish and koi, but note that it can prove harmful to other pool fishes, in particular golden orfe.

Long-term pool treatment at 0.25–0.5 ppm or 1–2 g per 4000 l.

To remove and control the evolution of parasites, excluding protozoa, this insecticide is used as a long-term pool treatment. Apply once every two weeks for six weeks at water temperatures of 10°–15°C and once every week for three weeks with water temperatures of 18°–20°C.

(*Note:* At 0.5 ppm metrifonate will reduce the quantities of zooplankton.)

Oxolinic acid

This antibiotic is used for treating bacterial infections and can be conveniently administered by adding it to goldfish food in a ratio of 2 g per kg of pellet food (divide if necessary).

Thoroughly mix the oxolinic acid and goldfish pellets in a clean, dry bowl and add 20 ml of sunflower seed oil per kilo of food to adhere the oxolinic acid to the pellets. Feed these to the fish, replacing the normal quantity of food, once a day for seven days.

Mercurochrome

This antiseptic is sold under various brand names as a 2 per cent solution. It can be used to disinfect damaged or infected areas on goldfish by application to a clean, dry surface using a cotton bud. Be careful not to allow the mercurochrome to enter the mouth or gill covers of your fish.

Chloramine 'T'

This antiseptic is particularly active against bacterial infections of the gills and skin. Used in short-term baths of one hour, its activity and success depend largely on its concentration being exact in relation to the pH level and hardness of the water used in the short-term bath.

The pH level and general hardness (GH) can be determined by using simple test kits. Once the pH and GH of the water are established, use the chart below to find the correct dose.

pH	Soft water	Hard water
6.0	2.5 ppm	7 ppm
6.5	5 ppm	10 ppm
7.0	10 ppm	15 ppm
7.5	18 ppm	18 ppm
8.0	20 ppm	20 ppm

Chloramine 'T' comes in powder form, and to obtain the correct ratios needed for treatments by using ordinary letter scales, apply the following method.

Measure out 10 g of chloramine 'T' and mix with 1 l of water (divide if necessary). Use the solution as follows:

Short-term bath at	10 ppm, 5 ml	per 5 l of water
Short-term bath at	15 ppm, 7.5 ml	per 5 l of water
Short-term bath at	18 ppm, 9 ml	per 5 l of water
Short-term bath at	20 ppm, 10 ml	per 5 l of water

(*Note:* It is very important that the water used in the short-term bath is free from dissolved or solid organic matter. **Caution!** This product is not toxic to fish, but do not use chloramine 'T' when formalin is present.)

WATER VOLUME IN LITRES

Some short-term treatments are followed up by a long-term treatment. In order to do this correctly, you will need to know the exact volume of water in your pool or aquarium in litres. For a square or rectangular volume of water, multiply in centimetres the length by the width by the depth and divide by 1000. To calculate the volume of a circular pool in litres, multiply the radius by the radius by the average depth and multiply by 3.14. Divide the total by 1000.

TREATING FOR PARASITE INFESTATIONS

During all treatments the water used should be the same temperature as that of the pool or aquarium. Ideally, for short-term baths the pool or aquarium water itself should be used, except in the case of a treatment using chloramine 'T', where clean fresh water will be necessary. All receptacles used for short-term baths should be aerated and covered to stop the fish from jumping out.

Trichodina, Costia and *Chilodonella*
Short-term bath (30 minute) 1 ml formalin per 5 l of water with malachite green at 2 ppm.

Apply long-term treatment of 15 ml formalin per 1000 l of pool water or 1.5 ml formalin per 100 l of aquarium water. Repeat long-term treatment after two days.

Ichthyophthirius multifiliis (white spot)
Short-term bath (30 minutes) 1 ml formalin per 5 l of water with malachite green at 2 ppm.

Apply long-term treatment of 15 ml formalin per 1000 l of pool water or 1.5 ml formalin per 100 l of aquarium water. Repeat long-term treatment after two days and once a week for four consecutive weeks.

Gyrodactylus and Dactylogyrus
Short-term bath (30 minutes) 1 ml formalin per 5 l of water with malachite green at 2 ppm.

Apply long-term treatment of metrifonate at 0.25 to 0.5 ppm or 1 to 2 g per 4000 l. Repeat long-term treatment every two weeks for six weeks with pool water at 10°–15°C and each week for three weeks if at 18°C or more.

For long-term aquarium treatment, use formalin at 1.5 ml per 100 l of water and repeat each week for two weeks.

(*Note:* Repeat short-term bath if fish becomes reinfested.)

Lernaea (anchor worm)
Remove attached worms by pulling gently with a pair of tweezers. Dab affected spot with mercurochrome.

Apply long-term pool treatment of metrifonate at 0.25–0.5 ppm or 1–2 g per 4000 l of pool water every two weeks for six weeks with pool water at 10°–15°C and every week for three weeks with pool water at 18°–20°C or more. If necessary or as a further precaution, feed fish on pellet food that has been treated with antibiotics.

Argulus (fish louse)
Remove the lice and dab mercurachrome on the spot from where they were removed. Apply the same long-term treatment as for *Lernaea*.

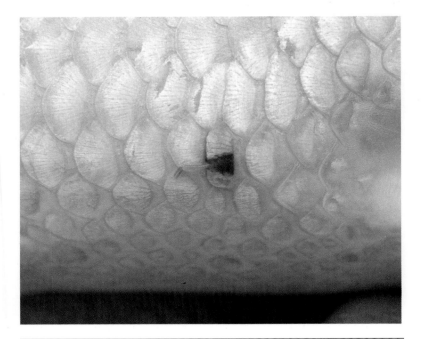

In some cases the area around the attached anchor worm will become infected.

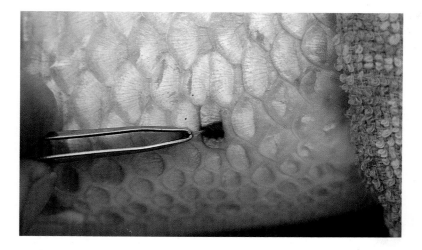

Remove the attached worm by pulling gently with a pair of tweezers towards the rear of the fish.

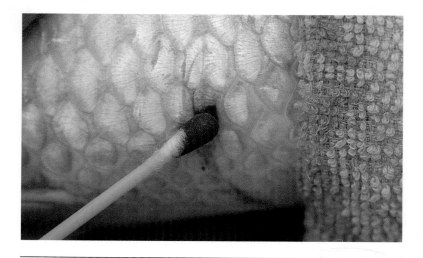

As a precaution, the area where the worm was attached should be swabbed with mercurochrome.

Ergasilus (gill louse)

Short-term bath (30 minutes) 1 ml formalin per 5 l of water with malachite green at 2 ppm.

Apply long-term treatment as prescribed for *Lernaea* and *Argulus,* including precautionary measures using food treated with antibiotics.

BACTERIAL INFECTIONS

See oxolinic acid and chloramine 'T', above.

FUNGUS GROWTH

Carefully remove any fungus growth or *Saprolegnia* by using a cotton bud soaked in a 0.1 per cent solution of malachite green.

Place affected fish in a short-term bath containing malachite green at 2 ppm for one hour.

Further Reading

Book

Dick Mills *Keeping Goldfish: An Aquarium Guide* Blandford, London, 1985 (Revised edition, 1990)

Periodicals

Aquarist and Pondkeeper (Monthly. Dog World Publications, 9 Tufton Street, Ashford, Kent TN23 1QN, UK)
Practical Fishkeeping (Monthly. EMAP Pursuit Publications, Bretton Court, Bretton, Peterborough PE3 8DZ, UK)

This pair of black Oranda goldfish have good finnage and excellent head growth, giving them plenty of individual character.

The Tosakin is a very special variety and is bred around the town of Kochi in Japan. Its development is mainly due to breeding and rearing in shallow water.

INDEX

All photographs are by Peter Cole, apart from those on pages 107 and 108, which are by M. Dorsan and S. Chilmonczyk.

THE ART OF
GOLDFISH KEEPING

Peter Cole

BLANDFORD

This book is dedicated to Audrey and Gilles Baschet

Also by the same author
The Art of Koi Keeping

A BLANDFORD BOOK
First published in the UK 1995 by Blandford
A Cassell Imprint
Cassell plc, Wellington House
125 Strand, London WC2R 0BB

Distributed in the United States by Sterling Publishing Co., Inc
387 Park Avenue South, New York, NY 10016-8810

Distributed in Australia by Capricorn Link (Australia) Pty Ltd
2/13 Carrington Road, Castle Hill, NSW 2154

British Library Cataloguing-in-Publication Data
A catalogue entry for this title is available from the British Library

ISBN 0-7137-2451-X

Typeset by Method Limited, Epping, Essex, UK
Printed and bound in Hong Kong

CONTENTS

Conversion Table

4.56 l	= 1 imperial gallon (3.78 l = 1 US gallon)
0.56 l	= 1 imperial pint
1 l	= 1000 ml
1 ml	= 1 cc or 20 drops from a standard eye-dropper
1 ppm	= 1 part per million
1 ppm	= 1 mg in 1 l of water
1 m	= 39.27 in
1 m	= 3.28 ft
1 m	= 100 cm
1 ft	= 30.48 cm
1 in	= 2.54 cm
° centigrade ÷ 5 × 9 + 32 = ° Fahrenheit	

PREFACE

Family pets are one of our first steps to introducing children to the wonders of nature. By developing their awareness and love for animals we are also helping to preserve the wonders of the world's natural resources, which are so often devastated, either by ignorance or by accident. These may be strong words to introduce a book on goldfish, but all is relative and they too are very much our family pets. They are beautiful creatures with much individual character. It is hoped that this book will help the reader to understand the art of keeping goldfish, and that your efforts will be rewarded with the beauty and pleasure that they can bring.

1

A History of Goldfish

Goldfish are probably among the world's most popular pets, and through the appearance of mutations, selection, cross-breeding and line breeding many different varieties exist today. The oldest records refer to goldfish as *Chin-yii* and they were discovered in China as early as the eleventh century in the form of poetry describing the beauty of these golden fishes. This confirms that they have existed for more than a thousand years.

They were believed to have originated from mutant common crucian carp with coloured scales. At one time they were also called golden carp and thought to be a mystical fish which people were absolutely forbidden to catch. It took several hundred years before the Chinese recognized them as being ornamental and during the Sung dynasty the emperors started to build garden pools in which to keep them. Caring for the goldfish became the work of the emperors' 'pisciculteurs', and this in turn started the evolution of breeding techniques and the appearance of the different varieties that are to be found today.

Their popularity stayed with the privileged for a long time until their recognized potential inspired the creation of breeding centres that brought them within the reach of all Chinese people. Eventually, goldfish keeping became something of a cult and they were bred in large numbers when an important breeding centre became established in Peking.

During the Ming dynasty, when ceramics became very popular, goldfish were bred in clay aquariums and kept in decorative ceramic jars as household pets. Many new varieties were created at this time by using artificial selection to produce variation in colours, double caudal and anal fins, telescope eyes, long fins and

Goldfish have been bred for more than a thousand years and their popularity is still growing.

shortened bodies. It was also in this period that the glass goldfish bowl was conceived. However, the Ming ceramic jars, containing more than 300 l of water, were a far healthier environment than the now obsolete glass goldfish bowl, containing at the most 3 to 4 l.

Goldfish were first introduced into Japan during the sixteenth century, when they were raised in the town of Osaka. They became popular at first with the aristocracy and the rich samurai. Then, at the beginning of the eighteenth century, they became popular with all Japanese people when important breeding centres were established in Nagoya and Koriyama. It was at this time that the Japanese developed advanced breeding methods that created more varieties. Bubble Eyes, Celestial, Pearlscales, Blue and Lionhead goldfish were all established during this period.

At the end of the eighteenth century goldfish were eventually introduced into Europe and the USA, and were finally classified zoologically. Although several names had already been recorded, which had caused some confusion, they were given the name, *Carassius auratus*, and therefore finally recognized for what they actually were from the beginning – a sub-species of the crucian carp, *Carassius carassius*.

The choice of aquarium is one of the most important aspects. The larger, the better!

2

EVOLUTION AND CLASSIFICATION

Kingdom Animalia
Family Cyprinidae
Genus *Carassius*
Species *auratus*
Name *Carassius auratus*

The scientific proof of the goldfish being a sub-species of the crucian carp was discovered during genetic research, when the two fishes were found to have the same number of chromosomes. The relationship between the two was confirmed when a certain percentage of offspring, during the specific breeding technique of pure line breeding, were seen to revert back to crucian carp. One apparent physical difference is in the formation of the dorsal fin, with that of the crucian being convex and that of the goldfish concave.

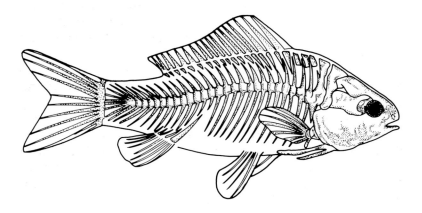

A typical goldfish skeleton (after Shiro Shindo)

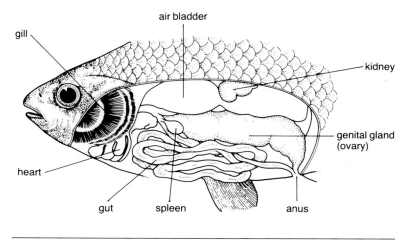

The location of goldfish inner organs (after Shiro Shindo)

One apparent sign of evolution can still be observed during the development of all young common goldfish bred today and that is their colour change. After they are born the transparent goldfish fry turn a brownish/olive green, as did their wild ancestors, and at a further stage their colour changes to a matt black, with a bluish hue, before their colour changes first to yellow and eventually to orange or red.

By careful observation, the offspring of the first crucian carp to appear with a golden reflection were repeatedly selected and bred until a perfect golden red carp was produced.

The development of the first fancy varieties of goldfish started with the discovery of the double anal fin, which came about by the splitting of the anal fin ray, with each developing its own membrane. This is not at all uncommon in the *Cyprinidae* family. Indeed, I have observed a double anal fin and the absence of ventral fins on Japanese Koi (*Cyprinus carpio*).

The hybridization and multiplication of all varieties of goldfish is possible because, unlike most hybrids in the animal world, their offspring are not sterile. Thus, selection of mutations, cross

Although the first goldfish were found in China, they have also evolved in other countries, such as Japan, where they have become a part of everyday life. In Tokyo two schoolboys, while having their lunch, admire a superb collection of fancy goldfish at the Tokyo Tower aquarium.

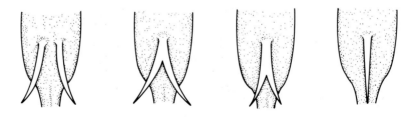

Four types of anal fin

14

and selective breeding created new varieties of goldfish with changes in finnage, body shape and, in some cases, unusual growths over the head and around the region of the eyes.

The common goldfish has five sets of fins, a tail fin known as the caudal, a dorsal fin, a pair of pectoral and ventral fins, and an anal fin. The fancy varieties of goldfish display variations in their finnage, the most apparent being the caudal fin which can be doubled, tripled or, in some cases, quadrupled. Each fin is made up of soft membranes that are fixed to an articulate hard fin ray situated at their leading edge.

As mentioned above, the variation in the fins appears with the splitting of the fin ray during the early stages of the development of the embryo. This phenomenon occurs only with the caudal and anal fins. Changes to the other fins are in their length or, as in some varieties such as the rancho, buffalo head or bubble eye, the total absence of the dorsal fin altogether.

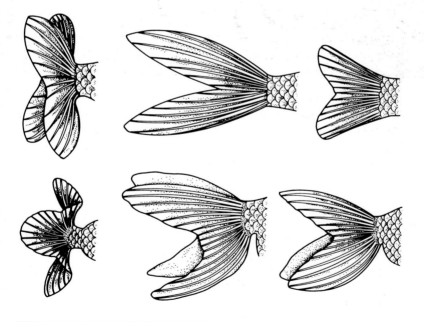

Six types of caudal fin

An aquarium containing fancy goldfish can create a colourful moving picture, both relaxing and pleasing to the eye.